Licensed to feel

Zaibah Iqbal

BookLeaf
Publishing

India | USA | UK

Presentation by *BookLeaf Publishing*

Web: www.bookleafpub.com

E-mail: info@bookleafpub.com

ISBN: 9789358316919

First edition 2023

DEDICATION

To all the anxious overthinkers out there,

This dedication is for you, the ones whose minds are always racing, analysing every detail, and imagining the worst-case scenarios. Your minds are like whirlwinds, constantly spinning with thoughts and worries. But know that you are not alone.

This dedication is a reminder that your anxiety does not define you. Your overthinking is a testament to your deep empathy and sensitivity. Embrace the fact that you see the world through a unique lens, one that allows you to notice the smallest details and understand the intricacies of human emotions.

Remember, it's okay to take a step back and breathe. Practice self-compassion and remind yourself that you are doing your best. Seek solace in the moments of stillness and find comfort in the knowledge that you are not alone in this journey.

You have a strength within you that shines through even in the midst of anxious thoughts. Embrace your resilience and know that you are capable of overcoming any challenge that comes your way. Trust in your ability to navigate through the twists and turns of life, even when your mind tries to convince you otherwise.

So, dear anxious overthinkers, keep pushing forward, knowing that your unique perspective and strength make you a force to be reckoned with. Embrace your journey, embrace your feelings, and never forget that you are worthy of love, understanding, and peace.

ACKNOWLEDGEMENT

First and foremost, I want to express my deepest appreciation to my family and friends for their endless love and belief in me. Your constant encouragement and understanding have been my guiding light throughout this creative journey.

To my fellow poets, thank you for inspiring me with your words and guiding me to explore the depths of my own creativity. Your wisdom and guidance have shaped my poetic voice and helped me find the courage to express my deepest feelings.

I am incredibly grateful to my publisher and the entire team behind the scenes who have worked tirelessly to bring this book to life.

Last but certainly not least, I want to extend my heartfelt thanks to each and every reader who has picked up this book. Your willingness to embark on this poetic journey means the world to me. It is my hope that my words touch your hearts and resonate with your own experiences.

Thank you for being a part of this poetic adventure.

PREFACE

Here we are again. We've all been there. Sitting alone, letting our thoughts drift away with themselves, as our cup of coffee runs cold. 2am talks with the moon hoping your overthinking will drift away soon.

As I sit here, pen in hand, I can't help but feel a mix of excitement and nervousness.

Through heartfelt verses and evocative imagery, you will experience the raw beauty of love, the ache of heartbreak, the warmth of joy and the turbulence of sorrow. Each page is a lyrical expression that will touch your heart and leave you with a renewed sense of connection to the power of emotions.

So, get ready and immerse yourself in the captivating rhythm of these poems and let them take you on an intimate journey of your own feelings.

Like menthol, like peppermint.

Coffee stains my windowpane as I observe the
thrashing of the rain,
The tide must be high over at Blackpool beach
as the icy winds roar.

I can almost smell the metal of the streetlights
quiver in the rashness of the storm,
A great calamity before the calm hits us again
once more.

I tuck my knees in high and tilt my head to the
cold window with its sparkling, trickling beads.

Everything is moving so fast outside right now
in this very moment, balancing my steady
heartbeat inside my chest, almost in perfect
harmony.

I place my hand against the window, the warmth
ripped away instantly,
Leaving a violent, electrifying buzz.

Like menthol, like peppermint.

The Last Letter.

There was this young man who I'd see every
morning on the way to college,
He'd nod back at me for each other we had
acknowledged.

An old friend he was of mine, different from the
rest.

Quiet and mysterious but an enthusiast at heart,
Cricket was his favourite sport and he played it
like an art.

Day by day we'd exchange glances, and maybe a
smile or two,
Then one day his dad passed away, and our
friendship had too.

He packed up and got ready to leave our town
when I saw him last that day,
No satchel bag, no navy blue duffel, nor a glance
my way.

He carried only a broken heart which he carries
with him today.

Perfection.

Perhaps it isn't until the afterglow fades away
that you realise how much effort you put in.

Every ounce of blood, sweat and tears that went
into your graft that you start to recall.

Realising that it all went to waste and that you
could have used that time for other things, more
important things.

For what it was worth, at least you were happy
in that moment, focused on making a positive
change.

Eventhough now you know it changed nothing
for you, and it was for someone else.

Could you ever see it working out for you
again?

Time is of the essence more times than you
know, perhaps giving up isn't the only option.
Regain hope.

If for whatever reason you decide to leave things be, forgive yourself.
Only when you feel ready and the stars have aligned, you can try again.

Now you can take this moment and centre yourself. (You're doing everything just fine).

Sunset Laughter.

I'll pick up my six string and play a gentle tune,
The mood is calm and the sun's setting soon.
I'll stand at the balcony and watch it go down,
Clutching closely to my silky evening gown.

Everyone is happy, sitting on the ground,
The laughter all around is such a heartwarming
sound.
I seek for company until your eyes meet mine,
Blessed with love and life, this night will define.

I look at you and you take my hand,
My feet delving into the golden grains of sand.
I make my way down to accompany my friends,
The summer air stirs as the mellow sun
descends.

Your deep brown eyes bring a sense of warmth
to my heart,
The simplicity of your words take my breath
from the start.

"Would you like to walk with me?"
Was the question that lingered on your lips.

I replied "yes,"
That tug on my heartstrings was the feeling I missed.

Phantom Tears.

IT thinks IT's easy to be free.

The way IT strolls down the street, late at night, patrolling the alleyways, looking for an escape.

Why does IT keep doing this?

IT touches my cheeks with IT's warm palms, in comfort.

But I hate IT. I'm not used to this, why doesn't IT understand?

I don't want IT to be apart of me. We're not the same.

I don't know IT, yet IT sticks with me like IT thinks IT's needed?

You're not needed.

IT seeps out through me, uncontrollably and I can't stop IT.

Why can't I stop IT?

Royal Valentine.

The smell of your aftershave from your favourite
jacket,
Eating crisps from your favourite crisp packet.
The warm laughter and hum of conversation,
Finally breaking the ice after months of
anticipation.

We messed it up and we've fallen down,
You were my King but you've lost your crown.
You left your heart, you fled the town,
You left me standing in my dressing gown.

The next month I received a letter from you,
I'm guessing it was the best you could do.
You had written in your favourite pen,
Wishing we could stop and start again.

You know I found that picture of you,
That day when you lost your shoe.

The crinkles in your eyes with that smile on your
face,
But like a missing puzzle piece, you've lost your
place.

You've left my heart an empty space...

You're moving on and doing your own thing,
Without me underneath your wing.
That empty park where we sat on those swings,
It feels different now but the birds still sing.

And I still remember when you wrote then,
Wishing if we could "stop and start again."

Paper Silhouette.

10

She was broken,
From the cracks you could see.

She tried to hide them so well,
But the closest around could see.

Her eyes were dull from the nights she wept,
She wasn't a nobody but there were a little few
she kept.

She spoke with such fragility in which her every
crack would tremble,

She was falling apart, and the pieces of herself,
she could not assemble.

Tucked Away.

My troubles are always tucked away between
my teeth.

But I can feel them niggling to get my attention.

My troubles aren't big but they are weighted.

They've become comfortable with making
themselves at home.

Trouble follows me and I don't know how to tell
it to leave me alone.

I don't like your company.

If only I could brush you off, you'd become less
painful, less tormenting, less troubling.

Once I've dealt with you, I will flourish.

I will smile again.
A brighter, softer smile.

The First Rage.

I gave you something special and you took advantage of it.

You stole the best parts of me to create your own masterpiece.

You left with pieces that were mine, so in the long run wherever you will be so will I.

I gave you my patience and friendship but it wasn't enough.

We shared a mutual understanding but I lost you somewhere in the translation.

But what about the broken bits of poetry you left behind.

What am I supposed to do with these broken pieces of poetry that aren't even mine?

What do you do when your heart's in a million pieces, because you gave away the best parts of yourself to those you thought would help put you back together, but the pieces remain in their cold hands, too lonely to become whole again...

13

Flawed Daydream.

I'd love to trace your veins just to feel the gentle
pulses which lead to your kind, beautiful,
beating heart.

I'd love to hear the words you whisper as they
become the melody to fill the void when you're
not around.

I'd love to tell you the stories of my past just to
see the sparkle in your eyes and the sweetest
smile I have ever sought.

I'd love to spend hours with you walking in dark,
talking beneath the stars, about how faith keeps
us together.

I'd love to witness the silence when you are
angry just so you know I will feel it too.

I'd love to be the one who reminds you of the
good times, to comfort you and be beside you.

I'd love to learn how to love somebody like you.

Wild Storm.

The feather-like sensation as your scent lingers
on my skin.

Reminding me of the times we walked in the
park, those long summer nights.

Laying on your leather jacket, on the damp
green grass.

The humidity alone was insufferable.

But those warm, honey-brown eyes made
summer worth sweating for.

Every slow-motioned blink setting a new blaze
of desire when you looked at me.

But the nights stripped you away from me the
long hours you were away.

And I'm still thinking about the feelings you left
me with, it's such a cliche.

Melancholy Rush.

I want to be the ink in your skin, sinking deep within.
And just like that, when will you let me in?

The needle in your veins, giving power to the pain.
Happiness you gain from momentarily going insane.

Like a hug to heal, everything that you feel.
Wrap me up around your heart like a titanium shield.

From minimalist lines to vibrant hues,
Of self-expression so passionately pursued.

Symbols of memories bold,
Ink etched deep, your stories unfold.

Timeless Fantasy.

Summer's sun shines hot on my plump rosy cheeks, as I gaze into the clear blue sky with its occasionally drifting white dots.

The smell of fresh cut grass envelops my senses as I lay on the greenery beneath me, staining my dress.

With my spirits lifted and my mind at peace, the sound of the new day quickens.

I lay here in this meadow surrounded by its colourful garden of buttercups and daisies just to appreciate the simplicity of life.

I'm a lover of stars and of the night sky, before the biggest star lights up the whole world, to provide us with a warm welcome to a blessed new day.

I think I'll stay a little while longer until I'm ready to face the challenges that are to come my way.

But I'll be sure to lay here again soon and I'm
sure I'll meet you again too.

18

Warning signs.

How could you do it?

How did you manage to rip apart our friendship
like a scab that was healing us both.

You not only left me with broken heart, you left
me wondering why and if I was at fault
somehow. I wasn't.

I still need an answer.

I needed a friend at the time and so did you.

You clung to me like the fibres on my winter
coat, blocking out cold, keeping us both warm
until your brashness made like lightning and
struck me with burning ice in my chest, leaving
me frozen and confused.

How did it feel standing in front of everyone,
knowing how much pain you spread.

I tried to enjoy the misery on you, but I was
boiling with regret.

Sometimes it's not even the red flags we miss.

It's the feelings we can't forget.

Deadweight.

I am sinking through my bed sheets, sinking through my sorrows.

Holding onto passing air as I try to hold onto tomorrow.

I'm so heavy with my feelings, my heart is painfully full.

But to let myself sink and whimper, is too hard for me to do.

I fall harder and faster down a cold vast blackness, the only thing holding me is the deadweight of my darkness.

I'm going to keep falling, will I ever reach the end?

Will I tear through the darkness, or float upon its depth?

I'll keep myself bound by staying in this void.

And when I'm ready to awake and build a brand new me.

I'll remember the darkness as my friend.

Life like mine isn't easy.

Because most times, I'm barely even together.

But pain like mine only lasts, if the world lasted forever.

Iris Reverie.

When you sat on the footstep of our house in
that old Grecian valley, strumming the strings of
my falling heart.

I think I know how the flowers must have felt.

When the bronze sun poured onto the fields,
livening up the fallen roots, wakening them out
of their sweet haze.

I think I know how the flowers must have felt.

When the hot raindrops pelted softly against my
golden skin in the heat of 2pm, and you watched
as I smiled at you.

I think I know how the flowers must have felt.

To be loved,
To be adorned,
To be captivated by you.

Now I know how the flowers felt.

Juneberry Magic.

24

Caribbean cocktails and pink shrimps on the
barbie.
A getaway so colourful, it could blow your
mind.

Swaying green palm trees and nights out on the
hammock.
Each star had it's own story to share.

Painted nails dipped into the emerald ocean,
with squinting eyes looking up at the blistering
sun.

Nothing to burden the heart here, only warm
welcomes by the afternoon aroma of the sea.

Saltine crackers tingle the tongue and ice cold
smoothies drip like sweat.

Nothing to fear here and nothing to flee from.

"I am happy here."

White, cotton, light dress dancing in the oceans
breeze, simply astounded by the moonlights
evening greeting.

"Hello old friend, remember me? 2am rooftop
talks & 10pm tears."

My eyes speak to the moon.

"You have met me at a better place, a place in
which I'm healing. No one told me this freedom
existed until I surrendered. Now I'm missing
home so much, I think it's time to leave. Nothing
like this could change a person, but it has
changed how I used to feel."

Goodnight moon, goodnight stars, goodnight the
ocean breeze. You were responsible for all
things impossible because it was you who put
my worrying heart at ease.

Essay.

If I was your favourite topic, would you write me like an essay?

Would you start with a title and end with a conclusion?

Would you research thoroughly to construct your exact thoughts of me?

Would you double check and proofread and still not change a thing, no matter how tempted you were because you know I, too, am flawed?

Would you keep the rough draft to refresh your memory of how you first remembered me?

Authentic, honest and original.

The detailed descriptions and raw reality of my, "well, I'm not who I used to be."

Because if that really defined me, would you still write me the same way?

Would it urge you to research more because you know that I'm not what you are looking for?

Would you skip to the highlights of my life, to create the best part of your essay, so that you at least felt some comfort in knowing that there were some things we had in common?

Or, would you write my whole story, uncensored, regardless of which side of me you preferred, because realising that the whole of me, was the best part of loving me?

Blue pt. II.

Blue is the colour when I long for you.

It's when I wrap my scarf a little tighter around my neck, standing on the bridge, looking over at the river.

It's the gasp that leaves my mouth when it's swept away in the seething breeze.

It's my cold tears looking back to see it fly away into the sky.

It's the chill sent across my bare neck longing for the warmth that used to be there.

It's the spitting rain, wetting my cheeks, painting them blue.

It's the way I start to take the next step, knowing its one without you.

Serendipity.

Like the livewires buzzing with electricity,
My heart buzzed uncontrollably at each word
you said.

"Serendipity" - you left us to destiny.
It's the way I could feel you pulling me to you.
Like you wanted me to.
Static but soaring.

You told me about your heartbreak,
but it was only jealousy in mine.

But you sensed it, you felt it, you tried to change
the topic like it mattered.

I? mattered? to you?

Both of us were missing love in our lives and
finding it in each other.

So you told me to close my eyes and then on the
count of 5, "smile".

Only the two of us, in the universe, "because this
is serendipity."

But you left destiny,
Like you left us...

September's Lullaby.

You're my safe space and my warzone.

And boy did my foundations tremble when the
blast of goodbye touched my fingertips.

You shattered beneath my power as rage filled
your every crevice.
Creaking and crumbling.

You roared.
Your stature smashing into smithereens.

It pained me.
Breaking down the building that built me.

My home! My haven!

Hold on to me, I will fix you.

But you disappeared like dust, like ashes, and
the harder I held on to you, the faster you drifted
away.

Now there you are, imprinted.

In my mind,
In my land,
In the palm of my hand.

And I walked out of this rubble as a rebel.

You were my safe space and my warzone

And boy did our foundations tremble when the
blast of "goodbye" finally reached my trembling
lips.